THE SECOND DEATH OF PRISCILLA

Russell Davis

BROADWAY PLAY PUBLISHING INC
224 E 62nd St, NY, NY 10065
www.broadwayplaypub.com
info@broadwayplaypub.com

THE SECOND DEATH OF PRISCILLA
© Copyright 2004 by Russell Davis

First printing: September 2007
I S B N: 0-88145-357-9

Book design: Marie Donovan
Word processing: Microsoft Word
Typographic controls: Ventura Publisher
Typeface: Palatino
Printed and bound in the U S A

THE SECOND DEATH OF PRISCILLA was produced by Actors Theater of Louisville as part of the 2003 Humana Festival, opening on 25 March 2003. The cast and creative contributors were:

PRISCILLA . . . . Barbara Gulan
PETER . . . . Will Bond
SECOND PETER . . . . .Jon Held
JACQUELINE . . . . Graham Smith
ARAMANDA . . . . Jen Grigg
SECOND PRISCILLA . . . . Jenna Close
COQUELICOT . . . . .Katherine Hiler

Director . . . . Marc Masterson
Scenic designer . . . . .Paul Owen
Lighting designer . . . . .Tony Penna
Costume designer . . . . .Lorraine Venberg
Production stage manager . . . . Nancy Pittelman

Readings and development work at New Dramatists, N Y C; Classic Stage Company, N Y C; People's Light & Theater Company, Malvern, PA; Long Island University, C W Post Campus, NY

CHARACTERS & SETTING

PRISCILLA, *a person upstairs in her room*
PETER, *her friend*
JACQUELINE, *a fabulous person from a neighboring land*
ARAMANDA, *who lives in her body*
COQUELICOT, *who lives in her head*
SECOND PETER & SECOND PRISCILLA, *two juggler/dancers*

PRISCILLA's *bedroom, the big, blue sky outside, and a forest.*

Time: the present.

ACT ONE

Scene One

(A large, empty, blue space)

(A window frame with pale curtains hangs down from above)

(PRISCILLA sits in a chair. Nearby is a second chair.)

(Enter PETER. He carries a large, black suitcase, or trunk. He sets the suitcase down.)

(He looks at PRISCILLA.)

PETER: That's very beautiful, Priscilla.

(No response)

PETER: I like your dress. I like it very much.

(Pause)

PETER: I like the birds flying. All those birds in the air. On your dress.

(Pause)

PETER: May I join you? Can I sit?

(He sits in the second chair.)

PETER: Your grandmother told me you were sitting up here. She tells me you call your bedroom the big, blue space. You like to sit all alone. In this big, blue space.

(Pause)

PETER: I like your grandmother. How she repeats the things you say. They seem important to her.

(He gets up. He goes to the window. He looks out.)

PETER: Nice, huh? I love this window. What you can see out there. I've always liked how you can see the woods. How they're perched up here with the house. On a cliff above the sea. A bluff. I like the rocks down below too. The sandy land. Sense of wilderness. I like it especially when there's wind. When a wind comes from other lands, like the big, bad breath of another planet, and those trees, the whole forest outside this house, bends. I like days like this too. I like all the sky. Nothing but big, blue sky.

(Pause)

PETER: Your grandmother says when you're not in here, you wander outside. Sometimes at night. She's had to go out and find you in the night.

(He goes back to his chair.)

PETER: Or she hears talking. You talk in here. Call out. Speak of things she's not heard before.

(Pause) She gave me a piece of paper. She found this paper one night. Outside your room. With words on it, or names.

(He takes out a piece of paper. He opens it.)

PETER: Aramanda. That's a word. Or name. Sounds like a boat. A ship from Palestine. Or Spain. Maybe a language. Sounds like a language we spoke. Aramanda.
   I want to ask you about all these words.
   In particular, this one, Crackle. When I saw Crackle on this paper right away I knew what it was. It's the word we used when we couldn't talk anymore. We'd say, Crackle. Which meant we'd have to stop again, talking. And the other person was meant to understand.

So you want to tell me about Crackle? Why it's here
on this paper?

Or how about Peter? You have my name here too.
You want to tell me how come my name's down here?
Close to Crackle?

Uh huh. How about Coquelicot? Is this a name,
Coquelicot? Some flower?

Or Jacqueline.

Who's Jacqueline?

(No response)

(PETER folds up the paper. He puts it in his pocket.)

(He goes to the suitcase. He opens it.)

PETER: I brought some things, Priscilla. A few things we
used to do together. For example, this. Remember these?

*(PETER takes a number of small, white balls from inside the
suitcase. He places them on the ground. He rolls them one
after the other past PRISCILLA.)*

PETER: You remember? You remember any of these?

(PRISCILLA pays no attention.)

(PETER walks past her. He collects the balls.)

PETER: You don't remember how we worked? All the
work we did. How much we had to practice?

(No response)

(PETER puts the balls back in the suitcase.)

PETER: Well, there're the balls. Some hats in there too.
Juggling rings. Juggling clubs. There's lots we used
to do in here. *(He takes out a juggling club. He spins it.
He drops it down to his foot. He kicks it back up into his
hand. He puts it back in the suitcase.)* I may just have to
practice, Priscilla. That's all. Right here. It's what I do
anyway. I could practice in front of you. Get to do my
practice today. Maybe you'll get to remember. Want to

practice too. *(Pause)* There were things you do, lots of
them, what you used to practice, I could never do some
of the things you do. To this day. You could dance too.
Play the violin. I remember you playing a violin. And
that's one thing I loved, Priscilla, about you. How
much you always wanted to practice. You wanted to
everyday. *(Pause)* Anyway. It's all in there. My suitcase.
Whenever you want to again. I got more too. Lots more
outside in the car.

(PETER *goes back to his chair. He regards* PRISCILLA.*)*

PETER: I guess, Priscilla. All the stuff I do with my body,
all my practice, the tricks, I guess I've begun to wonder,
deep down, if it doesn't seem arbitrary. This body. To
have hands. Or a face. Five fingers. Certain limbs which
work. Because there's something I'm not comfortable
with anymore. About this body. A longing now I can't
express. I don't know how. The most I can express is a
cage. I'm in a cage which I long to get out. And all the
tricks, these hard earned skills, are no longer enough.
They're like I'm banging now. Banging at the edge
of this cage. *(Pause)* I think of my body sometimes as
a horse. I ride this horse to get places. But there are
certain places I can't take the horse. I have to tie it to
a tree. Walk on up ahead. Just myself. No horse.
    And that's how I guess I think of you. Sometimes
that's the only way to approach you. Get to really talk.
If I have no horse. *(Pause)* It's thoughts like this I
learned from you. You're the thinker. I think I taught
you tricks and skills. You taught me thoughts. A way
to perceive. Like I was a creature, once upon a time,
responding only to what I could see. What was visible.
And I haven't seen you in some years, but this way you
taught to perceive, it's entered me, finally.
    Made me come back.
    Because I always felt there was a journey. A most
amazing journey you had to take. So I think I've come

to see if this is it. The journey. And if it is, I've come to wait. I'll be waiting, I guess, for when you come back. Sitting right here, reading. Or practicing. And if I do anything silly, like take your hand, or talk to myself, that's fine. I'm fine. I'm just waiting back here, that's all, at your point of departure. This place you last left.

(PETER *goes to the suitcase again. He takes out some juggling rings. He turns away from* PRISCILLA.)

(*Music*)

(SECOND PETER *appears upstage with a number of juggling rings. He juggles them.*)

PRISCILLA: Peter?

(*Music stops.* SECOND PETER *exits.* PETER *turns.*)

PETER: Yes?

(*Pause*)

PRISCILLA: I'm glad you're here, Peter.

PETER: Yes, I'm Peter.

PRISCILLA: Good.

PETER: Thank you. I'm glad too. (*He puts the rings back in the suitcase.*)

PRISCILLA: You okay?

PETER: What?

PRISCILLA: How are you? Are you well?

PETER: I'm fine. Thank you.

PRISCILLA: I'm fine too.

PETER: Good.

(*Pause*)

PRISCILLA: What is it, Peter?

PETER: What's what?

PRISCILLA: You look like you have something to say.
To tell me.

PETER: You have a very beautiful dress, Priscilla.

PRISCILLA: Hm?

PETER: Your dress. I like it.

PRISCILLA: Yes?

PETER: All the birds, yes. Flying into the air on your
dress. I like that.

PRISCILLA: Oh. I hadn't noticed.

PETER: It's nice.

PRISCILLA: Thank you.

PETER: You're very welcome.

(Pause)

PRISCILLA: It's lovely, Peter. Some of the things you say.

PETER: What things?

PRISCILLA: Well, about the horse. I loved you talking
like that. About a horse.

PETER: You heard me?

PRISCILLA: Oh, yes.

PETER: What else did you hear?

PRISCILLA: Just the horse.

PETER: Nothing else?

PRISCILLA: Well, no, you said a journey. Something
about a journey. But I didn't hear. I was still thinking
about the horse. How you leave it sometimes. To get
on ahead. *(Pause)* What are you looking at?

PETER: Nothing. Your room.
   I haven't seen it in a while. This room.

PRISCILLA: Yes. It's still here.

PETER: Yeah, I can see. Can see all the brick wallpaper still here. From when you lived at home.

PRISCILLA: I took it down.

PETER: What?

PRISCILLA: I took some of the brick down over there.

PETER: That's right. You did.

PRISCILLA: I scraped it off. It was peeling.

PETER: Right.

PRISCILLA: Maybe it should be different wallpaper in here.

PETER: You think so?

PRISCILLA: I don't know. It's been up so long.

PETER: I guess.

PRISCILLA: Yes, I'd like to take it all down. Sweep it away. It's not doing anything, this wallpaper.

PETER: What would you put up instead?

PRISCILLA: I'm going to paint a gate. A picture of a gate.

PETER: On your wall?

PRISCILLA: Yes, there should be some kind of gate. Which I could go through. When I want to think about what it could be like outside. But also for when I come back. I want a gate. Something I can close behind.

PETER: What's the matter with the door downstairs?

PRISCILLA: Hm?

PETER: For going outside.

PRISCILLA: I'd rather have a gate, that's all. In my room.

PETER: Okay.

PRISCILLA: You don't think my own gate would look nice?

PETER: Sure, of course, it could. You could paint a beautiful gate, I know, on these walls.

PRISCILLA: Well, that's all, Peter. I'd just like something like that. Something I can shut. So I can sit safe in here.

PETER: You don't feel it's so safe here?

PRISCILLA: I guess so. I guess I can be safe.

PETER: Good.

PRISCILLA: But I'd still like to do that, wouldn't you? We could do that together, Peter. Get out some paints. And put a gate right there in the corner.

PETER: Okay, sure.

PRISCILLA: Yes, where the brick was peeling.

PETER: Sure, Priscilla. We can do that. We can paint a gate for you in here.

PRISCILLA: Good. Thank you, Peter.

(PETER *goes back to his chair.*)

PRISCILLA: I've been writing a speech, Peter.

PETER: You have?

PRISCILLA: Yes. I'm almost done with it.

PETER: What's the speech?

PRISCILLA: I can't tell. You'll laugh.

PETER: No, I won't.

PRISCILLA: Yes, you'll think it's funny. You'll tease me.

PETER: You like to be teased.

PRISCILLA: Not this time, no.

PETER: Fine. I didn't think your gate was silly.

PRISCILLA: What gate?

PETER: The one you wanted. Right here in the wall.

PRISCILLA: Oh.

PETER: So tell it to me. I want to hear your speech.

PRISCILLA: No, it's not finished.

PETER: Then say the beginning.

PRISCILLA: I can't.

PETER: Come on, we've said silly, unfinished things to each other before. It's why we like each other.

PRISCILLA: It's spoken by a wolf.

PETER: What?

PRISCILLA: It's a wolf speaking. In my speech.

PETER: What wolf?

PRISCILLA: Well, the wolf, you know. Who wanted to eat the three pigs.

PETER: Oh, really? That wolf?

PRISCILLA: You think that's silly?

PETER: Well, no, I didn't hear it yet.

PRISCILLA: I'm sorry it's so silly.

PETER: Hey, no, I make up crazy things to say. All the time.

PRISCILLA: Like what?

PETER: You just heard a whole speech. About my body. I called it a cage. I said my body was a horse. I had to leave this horse. When I come to visit with you.

PRISCILLA: That wasn't silly.

PETER: Well, sure sounded it to me. Sounds like the same old silly Peter. In your presence. All over again.

So I think you should tell me right now. About this silly wolf. Get it off your chest, you know. I want to hear the speech. The beginning of a whole speech you're working on. To be spoken by a wolf.

(PRISCILLA *gets up. She goes to the suitcase.*)

PRISCILLA: Is this your suitcase?

PETER: What?

PRISCILLA: You brought a suitcase to me?

PETER: Yes. Yes, I brought a whole suitcase.

PRISCILLA: Can I look inside?

PETER: Of course, sure. Take a look.

(PRISCILLA *looks inside.*)

PRISCILLA: Peter?

PETER: Yes?

PRISCILLA: I can't see in here.

PETER: What? What can't you see?

PRISCILLA: I can't see what you've brought.

PETER: Come on. Of course you can see.

PRISCILLA: No, Peter. There's nothing here.

PETER: What?

PRISCILLA: Sssh.

PETER: What for?

PRISCILLA: *(Afraid)* I can't talk anymore.

PETER: You can't?

PRISCILLA: No, I'm sorry. I can't.

PETER: But we just got started.

PRISCILLA: I've got to go, Peter.

PETER: No, we're talking.

PRISCILLA: I have to, I'm sorry.

PETER: Where? Where are you going?

PRISCILLA: Crackle.

PETER: What?

PRISCILLA: *(Distracted)* Crackle's coming.

PETER: No, wait. Priscilla, wait!

*(PRISCILLA goes quickly back to her chair. She sits.
She withdraws.)*

(The sound of a creature walking across the wet sand.)

(PETER hears it. He looks out the window.)

(A shadow, or cloud, passes across the stage. PETER sees it.)

(He looks at PRISCILLA.)

PETER: Priscilla?

(Blackout)

(The sound of a galloping horse)

Scene Two

(The empty, blue space)

(The two chairs and suitcase are gone.)

*(A huge window frame, about twelve feet high, and seven
across, has replaced the small window which hung down
from above. This frame stands upright on the ground.
Pale curtains billow in it.)*

*(Enter JACQUELINE through the window curtains. She has
a full head of white hair, like a grandmother, or frumpy
godmother, except her face seems younger, and masculine.
She wears an ill fitting dress or nightgown.)*

(She comes downstage.)

JACQUELINE: *(To audience)* Nice, this curtain, don't you think?

This billowing one. In the large window here.

It makes me very happy. Makes me think so many things, a curtain like that. It's like a veil. A wifty thing. A shadow perhaps between us. Because I live the other side. In a land of endless, empty expanse. And you live here. In a place of tiny, particular things. We're like neighbors. This curtain is our fence. We have a tiny, flimsy fence between us. Through which we can catch a glimpse of each other. Take a peek. Maybe even get to speak. Like now. Because I find it hard, yes, for us to be neighbors. We have such differences. Hardly ever see each other. In fact, most of what I do is invisible to you. Unsuspected. And what seems so visible to you makes little sense to me. *(Pause)* You can call me Jacqueline. If you should find yourself close again sometime to our fence, our little window here, call out Jacqueline, Jacq, and I will answer. From a land you cannot go to. A place you could never ride to, no, not on a horse. *(Pause)* I'm trying to remember the first time I saw Priscilla. The first glimpse she caught of me. *(Pause)* I think a physical perception of life, this world you see out here, is like a straw house. Or a house of sticks. Something you built. And I think that's when Priscilla first caught a glimpse of me. When she could see how flimsy these things were, what we build, what we believe we can see. *(Pause)* I think sometimes of what's out here as surface. Little sand castles. And the other side where I live are invisible depths, and waves, beneath. The real influence. And I think of children. How they see monsters. Until it's explained we don't see monsters. We're civilized.

And so these monsters become no longer seen. Though we're all sure they're still there. Right beneath the eyes. Huge ones, yes, as big as you can make or

suppress them in your mind. I know. I've seen them.
How they can walk right through under everything you
say. And I think of myself as what might be like a lion
tamer to you. I am here perhaps to show your monsters.
To parade them before your eyes. Make them do their
tricks for you.

(Sound of someone, or thing, walking across wet sand.)

JACQUELINE: For example, we have a wolf. Which is
not like any wolf you could ever see this side of our
window. This wolf has no sense of physical limitation,
no understanding of how a wall, or the door to a house,
is meant to keep him separate from getting to us. This
wolf walks on ceilings at night. Likes to stare down at
you. He can come from nowhere, like the wind. The
big, bad breath of another planet. All things blow aside
in his path. And where this wolf lives a day is like a
thousand years, and there's no brick on earth, what
can withstand a day or two like that.
    And this wolf has words for you. He can speak.
Whole speeches. He can tell you what you see out here,
as a wolf, is the bare tip of what a wolf can really be.

(A shadow, or cloud, passes across the stage.)

JACQUELINE: Priscilla hears this wolf. She has. All his
nimble words. Prowling outside her room. Waiting for
her to fall asleep.

(The sound of a galloping horse)

JACQUELINE: But I think there's nothing to be so afraid
of. Really. In this land I speak from. This place I tell.
We're neighbors, I said. We have the same fence, the
same dark forest, our back yards are next to each other
under the same big, blue sky. And I think I should
come over more often. I should beckon to you. Pull
aside this veil sometime. Let you know who I am.

(JACQUELINE *reaches to pull aside a curtain. Her dress parts slightly. It reveals the hind leg of a* WOLF.)

JACQUELINE: *(To audience)* I just love this curtain, don't you? This window here where Priscilla sits. Through which I can come out to you.

(The curtains continue to billow.)

(Blackout)

Scene Three

(The big, blue space. There are streaks of yellow.)

(The huge window frame is gone. Instead, a small window hangs down again from above. The window is closed.)

(A young girl, ARAMANDA, *sits in the chair where* PRISCILLA *sat.* ARAMANDA *has short cropped hair and wears an eyepatch. Her face is dirty and scarred. She wears the same dress* PRISCILLA *wore.)*

*(*PETER *sits in the other chair. He is asleep, holding an open folder in his lap. Nearby is his suitcase.)*

(There is a silhouette of a large horse grazing upstage.)

*(*ARAMANDA *watches the horse.)*

ARAMANDA: *(Whispering to* PETER) Is that your horse?

(No response)

ARAMANDA: Is that your horse out there? In the big, blue space?

*(*PETER *remains asleep.)*

*(*ARAMANDA *gets up and goes to* PETER. *She takes the folder from his lap. She looks at it. She closes it and puts it back. She reaches into one of his pockets. She takes out a folded piece of paper. She crumples it and puts the paper in her own pocket.)*

(She goes back to her chair. She sits.)

ARAMANDA: *(To* PETER*)* I asked you, Is that your horse?
Did you come here on that horse?

*(The silhouette of the horse moves upstage. It comes to a stop.
It grazes again.)*

*(*ARAMANDA *watches the horse.)*

*(*PETER *wakes up. He sees* ARAMANDA*.)*

PETER: Priscilla?

(No response)

*(*ARAMANDA *continues to watch the horse.)*

PETER: Priscilla, I'm sorry. I fell asleep. *(He looks down at
his lap.)* I fell asleep looking through this folder. I found
it open. Right here in the room. I wondered if you left it
open for me. You have stories in here, Priscilla. I never
knew you were thinking about these stories. All these
thoughts. *(Pause)* Would you rather I didn't then?
Look at any thoughts you have, Priscilla? In this folder?

(No response)

PETER: I can tell you, actually, what I saw in here.
It's not much. Cause what I saw started me thinking.
All my own thoughts about you. And somewhere I got
tired. Real tired from driving here. Made myself fall
asleep. But I'd like it, I would, if you'd read sometime
from this folder. Some of the things in here.

(No response)

PETER: I guess not. *(He puts aside the folder.)*

ARAMANDA: Is that your horse?

PETER: Hm?

ARAMANDA: The horse. Did you come here on the horse
over there?

PETER: There's a horse?

ARAMANDA: Yes. It keeps moving. You really should tie it up better. What if it decides to come wander over here? You shouldn't ride up, you know, so closely on a horse.

(PETER *goes to the window. He looks out.*)

PETER: I don't see a horse. Any horse out there.

ARAMANDA: You don't see that horse?

PETER: No, what horse? I see the shore below, that's all. And the woods. The woods right here at the top of the cliff. The bluff. There's no horse.

ARAMANDA: You really shouldn't tease, you know.

PETER: What?

ARAMANDA: Or pretend like this.

PETER: I'm not teasing.

ARAMANDA: Then why are you saying you can't see a horse?

PETER: Because I can't.

ARAMANDA: I never met anyone before who couldn't see their own horse.

PETER: I don't have a horse.

ARAMANDA: Then how did you get here?

PETER: What?

ARAMANDA: I don't know how you could have gotten here. Except on a horse. Because if that's not your horse over there, then there has to be another one. Another horse to get here. And if that's true, there's another, then that means someone else is here. And I need to worry. Someone else too rode up on a horse.

(*The* HORSE *upstage moves. It stops.*)

(ARAMANDA *watches.*)

PETER: Priscilla, come on. Don't be in a strange mood with me, okay? I just woke up.

ARAMANDA: You're strange yourself.

PETER: What?

ARAMANDA: Calling me Priscilla.

PETER: You don't want that?

ARAMANDA: No. There is no Priscilla anywhere around.

PETER: No? Where is she?

ARAMANDA: How should I know?

PETER: I don't know. You sure look like her.

ARAMANDA: I do not.

PETER: You don't look like Priscilla?

ARAMANDA: No.

PETER: Then who do you think you look like?

ARAMANDA: I don't know who you think Priscilla should look like. But it's not me. I don't look at all like how you think a Priscilla should look like.

(PETER *sits in his chair. He regards* ARAMANDA.)

PETER: *(Gently)* Sure, you do. You look exactly like I think Priscilla should look. The same long, lovely, fair hair. Just like Priscilla. And the same pretty, pale face. Like you always had. Almost transparent. Like if I looked too hard I could see to the other side of you. And you have the same dress. This lovely, blue dress with birds on it. I just love how you sit in that dress, Priscilla. How you perch. Like you could fly away. Any moment. And your forehead too. I love that line down your forehead when you're thinking. Did you know that? Did I ever tell you? Your face gets all distant when you think like this. You make me feel like I'm out here, watching. In a world faraway from you. A whole different place. There seems so little of you left when you're in there thinking. You get so thin and frail. Like you could vanish, your whole body. Like if I tried to touch you, my hand would go right through. And all that's left is what's in your eyes. These same, big, wondering eyes. Full of things to think about. And when I take a look too, down your eyes, I swear I can see some other, even deeper person. Some other person you are, Priscilla, down there in your eyes.

(ARAMANDA *stands. She slaps* PETER.)

(*Pause*)

ARAMANDA: My eyes aren't big. Nor do they wonder. My eyes are small. And one is missing. I have an eyepatch. An eyepatch, yes, because it's not there anymore for me to see out of. There's nothing to see down here in my eyes. So don't lie to me, ever again, about my eyes. And don't tell me either I have long, lovely hair. My hair is short and crooked, And my face is not pretty pale. It is dark and ugly.

PETER: Your face is never ugly.

ARAMANDA: Oh, don't be so stupid. Of course it's ugly. It has four big scars right here across it.

PETER: What scars?

ARAMANDA: You can't see scars?

PETER: No. I do not see any of your scars.

ARAMANDA: You are such a liar.

PETER: No, I'm not lying. I do not see these scars on your face. I see no eyepatch. I can see none of this stuff you tell me now you can see.

(*Pause*)

ARAMANDA: How can you look at me and tell such a lie? How can you not see these scars right here on my face? *(She goes to the window. She looks out.)*

(Pause)

(PETER looks through his pockets.)

PETER: Priscilla? I had a piece of paper, Priscilla. Where is it? Your grandmother gave me this paper.
   Did you take away my paper? All the words I had, the names you wrote?

(No response)

PETER: Come on, Priscilla. There were words on that paper. Like Aramanda. Jacqueline. Like Crackle. You wrote down Crackle on this paper. Where is the paper, Priscilla?

(No response)

PETER: Fine. *(He goes to his suitcase. He opens it. He takes out three juggling clubs.)*

(The sound of a violin)

(PETER turns upstage away from ARAMANDA. He juggles the clubs.)

(The sound of juggling clubs landing in PETER's hands.)

(ARAMANDA watches.)

ARAMANDA: What is it you're doing?

(PETER doesn't respond.)

ARAMANDA: It sounds lovely, what you're doing.

(The big, blue space darkens. Then shifts to yellow)

(The sound of the violin and sound of PETER continue.)

(ARAMANDA goes to PETER. She stands next to him, watching.)

(The horse upstage moves away. It comes to a stop.)

(ARAMANDA *reaches out her hand. She takes one of the clubs.*)

(PETER *turns to her, holding the others.*)

ARAMANDA: Did, you see? Just now?

PETER: What?

ARAMANDA: The horse.

PETER: What about it?

ARAMANDA: It moved. It's moved all the way over there. Away from us.

PETER: Okay.

ARAMANDA: It may leave us soon. For good.

PETER: Okay, good.

(PETER *reaches to take back the third club.* ARAMANDA *holds onto it.*)

(*Music. The sound of a violin continues.*)

ARAMANDA: I know you don't think it's yours. The horse. You think it's mine. Whatever I see. And I don't want to argue. About some horse. But I think I better tell you. I should say how I appreciate, I do, you came here. You stopped by. Made this journey. All to find me. But it doesn't belong to you, no. A journey like this. To come so faraway. From any world you know. Any place you could ever live.

   And so if that could be your horse, if there's any chance, you should go over now and get it. Ride away, I know, from here. Because once the horse is gone, once it leaves, or something comes to take it away, there's no way left, you see. To escape from here. No way you could get out fast enough on foot. (*Pause*) Just a warning, that's all. I'm like a gatekeeper, you know. To the land ahead.

(PETER *takes* ARAMANDA'*s hand.*)

PETER: *(Softly)* Come, Priscilla.

ARAMANDA: Hm?

PETER: I want you to do this with me.

ARAMANDA: What? What will we do?

(PETER holds two clubs in his free hand.)

PETER: Let's do this together, Priscilla. Come on.
What we used to do.

ARAMANDA: It sounds so pretty when you call me that.

PETER: Priscilla, come.

ARAMANDA: So very pretty.

PETER: Come. Just throw the club.

ARAMANDA: Hm?

PETER: Throw it to me, yes. Toss it.

(Still holding her hand, PETER tosses a club to ARAMANDA with his other hand. She tosses one back to him. They juggle together, each using one hand.)

(The sound of a violin continues.)

(Upstage, the horse is gone.)

(Lights dim.)

(Two figures, SECOND PETER and SECOND PRISCILLA appear upstage. They dance together, passing clubs between them.)

(The sound of a chorus. Sound of an orchestra)

(The violin continues.)

(Blackout)

Scene Four

(The big, blue space)

(PRISCILLA is asleep in the chair by the hanging window. A violin rests in her lap.)

(The other chair is empty. PETER's suitcase is nearby. Three juggling clubs are lying on the ground.)

(JACQUELINE stands outside the closed window. She walks back and forth. She comes back to the window. She regards PRISCILLA through the window.)

(PRISCILLA wakes up. She sees JACQUELINE.)

JACQUELINE: *(Tapping on the window pane)* May I come in?

(No response)

JACQUELINE: I thought it would be good. If I came in. *(Pause)* I've been waiting out here for quite some time. I thought I could see you asleep. I thought if you awoke, I'd like to ask if I could come in. Make myself at home. Right in there where you are. *(Pause)* I know you've seen me before. It's not good to pretend like this. Not to speak to me. *(Pause)* I'm the one who told you there was a wolf. A wolf is coming. You wouldn't want me to get caught out here, would you? When the wolf comes?

(No response)

JACQUELINE: You know, I've always wondered about that. The words huff and puff. Why would a wolf ever say that? I will huff and puff. All your house down. Sounds demeaning to me. A wolf actually speaking like that. Besides, how could a wolf do that anyway? Blow a house down. That's simply not what a wolf does, how he frightens. And so I think if a wolf could

speak, I mean, if we live in a land now all around where
the wolf speaks, then why, I would like to know, would
the wolf say something like huff and puff your house
down? That's not what any wolf would speak to me.
I mean, not if I was meant to be frightened. By the
words of such a wolf.

You know what the wolf would speak? If it came
to me? I mean, if I happened to be passing through
some patch of land, a wilderness maybe, where if a
wolf looked at me I could hear it speak? All its words?

I think what the wolf would speak would be the word
bluff. That word. Not huff or puff. But bluff. And he
wouldn't mean a person who bluffs or misleads. No,
not at all. He'd mean like a cliff. A bluff, yes. A high,
steep and precipitous place. Where he would tell me
I have built my house. Overlooking a large body of
water. Like the sea. And he would want to know,
naturally, why I built my house in a place like that.
On a sandy bluff above the sea. Did I not know that
there could be a wind sometime? Winds will blow?
Rains will descend, floods come? And beat upon this
house?

Did I not know that?

Hadn't I been told?

And if I expected my house to survive perched like
this in the path of wind, rain, and all the flood, and if I
didn't expect the fall of my house to be very, very great
indeed, ruinous, in fact, then I should have built it, my
house, yes, on rock. Given it a good firm brick footing.
A foundation to count on. *(Pause)* Yes, I think those are
words I could hear a wolf speak. If it spoke to me.

And I think I can hear it further say to me that he'll be
waiting. That's all. Outside my house. For all this wind
and rain and flood to come up. He'll just be prowling
out there. Like a wolf. Prevent my leaving. Make me
stay in this house. This place I have built myself. On a

bluff like this. Above the sea. *(Pause)* That's how I think. Yes. How a wolf would speak. At least to me.

(PRISCILLA *stands. She goes to* PETER's *suitcase. She places her violin on top of the suitcase.*)

(JACQUELINE *follows her from a distance.*)

JACQUELINE: It's amazing. Amazes me how a few small details can get bollixed. Then add to the original bollix a couple of millennia and a whole story is distorted. Used as something to soothe our children. Because I think this little child's tale, with words like huff and puff, and the wolf who comes down the chimney, which a wolf cannot do, it's wind what comes down a chimney, not a wolf, and how can you boil wind in a pot of water, all of which proves my point that this story is a red herring. Something charming, yes, to distract us. From what really may have happened. Because I do believe there was indeed a wind. Lots of rain and flood too. And I believe there was a house which fell. And a wolf too. Just waiting outside, I know.

And I have to ask myself, I do, who was it, then, who changed this story? Bollixed the details. I mean, we assume it has a happy end. We assume history belongs to us. The victors. But what if somebody came along in the calmness after, after all the wind and rain and all the flood, and tampered with our story? Twisted it just a little. Made it slightly silly. So we wouldn't know, really, what happened. Take it too seriously. And so for the rest of our life here on earth, we'd tell this slightly skewed story to our children. Each one, as they grew up.

And when I think about this story in this light. That it's been tampered with, then I have to question its ending too. About the inhabitant in the brick house. I have to wonder is there really such an inhabitant around? Some moral like that which really, effectively exists?

Or is it actually the wolf? The wolf is still around.

Telling these stories? So we won't know where he is.
We can't see him. All the things he's up to.

(PRISCILLA *goes back to her chair. She sits.*)

(JACQUELINE *regards the violin on top of* PETER's *suitcase.
She regards the juggling clubs.*)

JACQUELINE: You have a friend. A visitor, I see. He's
come by. I can see his suitcase. All his stuff. I imagine
he'll be back soon enough. Be nice to have him here,
wouldn't it, for when the wolf comes?

I should like to meet him myself, I would. Stand right
there in that room with you and meet your friend. Yes.
I imagine I'll do that sometime. Be in that room and
meet your friend. But I must be off now, I'm afraid.
You wouldn't want me to get caught out here, would
you? When the wolf comes? (*She goes to the window. She
taps on it.*) By the way, will I find him here, your friend?
The visitor? If I come back, will he be visiting you here,
in your wonderful brick house? Or will he stop by
where Aramanda once did live? Or Coquelicot. Will
I find him in the forest with Coquelicot? In the house
where she did live?

It'd be an awful shame if your friend had to witness
that. What the wolf did to them. How the wolf tore
up the face of Aramanda. Took her eye out. And poor
Coquelicot. What he did to her. How he broke her
wing. How they fled, both of them, back to their
houses. And now they're all ready, yes, to be finished
off. Never had a choice, did they, living like they did?

(*No response*)

(JACQUELINE *taps on the window again.*)

JACQUELINE: But that's what I like about you. You're
smarter how you live. I can't imagine any connection.
Can't imagine what happened to them happening to
you. Nah. Because then I'd have to imagine I could be
all that's left. To be here, you know, in that room. Right

there where you sit. When the time is come, yes,
to meet your friend. *(She taps on the window again.)*

(A pane of glass cracks.)

(A large crack appears across the big, blue space behind.)

(JACQUELINE regards the window.)

JACQUELINE: Oooo, look. Look right there. It's a crack.
Imagine that. A crack in your window. I'm sorry. It's
a shame no matter where you live there's always got
to be a window. Always some spot to look through.
See what's coming. No matter what you do.

(Blackout)

Scene Five

*(A forest. The forest has a large crack crossing
indiscriminately through it.)*

(The window hangs as before. A pane of glass is cracked.)

*(COQUELICOT sits in the chair. She has wings, one of which
is clearly broken. She wears the same dress PRISCILLA wore.
She holds the violin in her lap.)*

*(Nearby are the other chair, PETER's suitcase, and some
juggling clubs.)*

(Enter PETER.)

PETER: Hi.

(COQUELICOT smiles.)

PETER: You okay?

(No response)

PETER: Listen, I'm sorry. I had to get out of here. Go
for a walk. You should do that too, I think. Get out and
walk. It's obsessive, Priscilla, how you want to stay in
here. You won't budge. Like you're some little girl

again, you can't leave this room. There's terror down
the hall. Some idiotic thing you can't get past. And
if you could talk to me sensibly about it, I would
understand, I could help. But I don't get it, Priscilla.
I can't help when everything you say seems so damn
elliptical. It's obsessive in here. I mean, at first, it's
exciting, wow, to come back to you again, everything
has extra added meaning, extra air, some other
perspective to each thing, each word we speak, like
it's all an allegory, a parable, all pointing to some great,
big depth below. Like we're these icebergs. This body
of mine is the tip of an iceberg, and you and I bump,
we slide past each other in all kinds of ways we can't
possibly see from here. The tip of an iceberg. But then
after a while, Priscilla, no, this is not fun anymore. At
all. This is just plain, damn complex, it's always been
between us, and I don't know how I decided to forget
all that, all what is complex, just so I could remember
this other free spirited thing, this dolphin you are,
bouncing up and down in the sea, slipping away under
the surface, coming back again from nowhere, like you
speak to me from other worlds. And much that I love
you, Priscilla, I do, I will always love you, I have to
mention this is not what I love about you. It's what
I forgot. This maddening obsessiveness you have
sometimes. This ridiculous extreme the other side
of you, and this is not anything I can like, or ever
did like it, when you get stuck like this on one damn,
stupid issue. When you circle like a moth around some
tiny flame. Some worthless campfire, which you should
just kick to pieces, and get the hell out of here. *(Pause)*
I'm better now. I went for a walk.

(Pause)

COQUELICOT: Come.

PETER: Hm?

COQUELICOT: I want to sit by you. Right here.
(She goes to a chair. She sits.) I'm sorry. I won't do
it again. Be obsessive. Like you say.

PETER: You can't help it, no, I'm sure.

COQUELICOT: No, it will never happen again.
To be obsessive. See? All gone.

PETER: *(Smiling)* Right.

COQUELICOT: I want you only to have all good
memories of me.

PETER: They are good.

COQUELICOT: No, no frowning allowed when you
think of me. No mothballs in the campfire. Only magic
moments, okay? Only magic forever.

PETER: Okay.

COQUELICOT: Good. And I will think the same of you.
Only magic. It's nothing now but magic. Each thought
I think of you.

PETER: Fine. *(He sits.)*

COQUELICOT: Good. So what can we talk about now?
That will be magic. That will enchant again. All your
memories of me. How can I be again for you like the
dolphin?

(COQUELICOT takes PETER's hand.)

COQUELICOT: Was I talking again? About the wolf?

PETER: It's okay.

COQUELICOT: Oh, I hate it. I'm sorry. It's not me when
I talk like that about a wolf.

PETER: I know.

COQUELICOT: You must just shoot me, that's all,
next time. Take a shot. Put away my misery. Because

I am nothing again if I am obsessive. I am become again like a horse, that's all, with a broken leg.

PETER: Oh, come on.

COQUELICOT: No, it's becoming now serious, I think. What can we do, do you think, to stop all this talk of a wolf?

PETER: I don't know.

(COQUELICOT *strokes* PETER's *cheek.*)

COQUELICOT: Do you tell me, Hush?

PETER: Yes. Yes, I do.

COQUELICOT: You smile and say, Sssh, all the wolf is gone?

PETER: Yes, I smile.

COQUELICOT: Good. I'm glad you smile. I'm glad you say hush for me. No more wolf.

PETER: Uh huh. I shout too.

COQUELICOT: No, you don't.

PETER: Yes. I really yell.

COQUELICOT: No. Why should I remember that? Your face when you yell? Please, never yell. Promise to just say, Sssh, tell me the wolf is gone. And I will listen.

PETER: No, come on.

COQUELICOT: Yes, it is only you and me, that's all. Together again. Sssh. Who cares now about a wolf? He is nowhere to be seen.

(*The sound of a gentle breeze in the woods.*)

COQUELICOT: Magic, yes?

PETER: Hm?

COQUELICOT: It feels like magic. To sit together like this. When there is no wolf. I like to hold your hand. I like to smile. Faraway from all this talk of a wolf.

PETER: Right.

(PETER *leans his head on* COQUELICOT's *shoulder. He closes his eyes.*)

COQUELICOT: You know, when I talk about a wolf, I have only your word for it. How I talk. And I trust it, of course, your word. Everything you say. But it is like if I should snore, in my sleep, and you should tell me I kept you up all the night, I was snoring. And I can only say, I'm sorry, that's not me, to do such a thing to you, to snore, and keep you awake all the night.

When I talk about the wolf, it's like that. I can't remember. I remember nothing when we are together like this. It is only magic to me. Every word I speak, I want to be magic for you. And every word you speak, I hear magic too. I can see no danger all around. There is nothing near, nothing faraway, to cause us trouble. *(Pause)* You know, when you tell me, when you come back like this with stories of a wolf, I think two things.

I have thought perhaps you heard yourself. You who talked like that. It is you who snored, and you wake yourself up, and think it was me, who snored.

Just kidding. You could never snore. You are way too perfect for me.

And what else I think is you will rescue me anyway. From this wolf. If he is real, somewhere faraway I cannot see, you will find where he lives. You will capture him. And if he is just a dream, you will also track him down and stop all our talking of him.

Because if he is real, or just a dream, he is still only a wolf. Who wants to take you away from me.

(Pause)

PETER: Would you do something for me?

COQUELICOT: Of course.

PETER: While you're in this mood.

COQUELICOT: Of course. What mood?

PETER: Read to me.

COQUELICOT: Read? Yes, what should I read?

PETER: Read to me, please. One of your stories.

COQUELICOT: What stories?

PETER: Come. I'll get the folder.

(PETER *stands. He gets the folder lying on top of the suitcase. He brings it to* COQUELICOT.)

PETER: Here. Read from this.

COQUELICOT: What's in here I should read?

PETER: I don't care. Just anything. Read.

(COQUELICOT *looks down at the folder.*)

PETER: You going to read?

COQUELICOT: Yes. Yes, I will read.

PETER: What's the matter, then?

COQUELICOT: Nothing, no.

PETER: No, you look troubled.

COQUELICOT: No, I'm just hoping, that's all.
You will like if I read.

PETER: Of course I'll like it.

COQUELICOT: Okay.

PETER: I've always liked it. Just read.

COQUELICOT: Okay.

(COQUELICOT *adjusts herself. She smiles to* PETER.
She opens the folder.)

(Pause)

PETER: What's the matter?

COQUELICOT: Hm?

PETER: I said, What's the matter?

COQUELICOT: I don't understand.

PETER: What?

COQUELICOT: What I am reading.

PETER: What's there to understand, come on, you wrote it.

COQUELICOT: I wrote it?

PETER: What?

COQUELICOT: This was written, yes, by me?

PETER: Yes. It's your handwriting.

COQUELICOT: Good. I'm glad I can be so clever sometimes.

PETER: You don't remember writing this?

COQUELICOT: No, I never remember when I am clever. I am not clever, in fact, at all.

PETER: Who wrote this, then? It's all your handwriting.

COQUELICOT: I don't know. You tell me. You are clever. You decide, please.

(Pause)

(PETER *takes the folder.*)

PETER: I'm sorry. We should do something else, Priscilla.

COQUELICOT: Hm?

PETER: For magic, I think.

COQUELICOT: Yes?

PETER: I think so, yes. Let's find something else for now. What would you like?

COQUELICOT: I'm happy, I told you. Just to sit here.

PETER: Fine, then, I'm sorry. Really. Let's do that, okay? Let's sit.

COQUELICOT: Good. I'm glad.

PETER: Okay, good.

(They sit together.)

(PETER reaches over. He takes COQUELICOT's hand.)

(The sound of a gentle breeze in the woods)

COQUELICOT: Magic, yes?

PETER: Hm?

COQUELICOT: It feels to me like magic. When we sit like this. I like when you take my hand again. When you take me faraway. From all this talk of a wolf. *(She smiles.)*

(Sound of a breeze getting stronger)

(Blackout)

Scene Six

(The big, blue space)

(The crack across it is wider now. There are dark streaks of yellow.)

(The window hangs as before. A pane is cracked.)

(The sound of a strong wind)

(ARAMANDA: sits in a chair. She wears PRISCILLA's dress. The scars on her face are wider, and she seems blind in her other eye. She has lost a leg.)

(Piled to one side, as if against a door, are the other chair, PETER's *suitcase, the violin, and juggling clubs.)*

*(*JACQUELINE *stands outside the window. She walks back and forth. She lifts her face. She breathes in the wind.)*

(She regards ARAMANDA. *She comes back to the window.)*

JACQUELINE: *(To* ARAMANDA*)* It's amazing, this wind, isn't it?

(No response)

JACQUELINE: The first time I heard this wind, I thought, amazing. You'd think nobody could hear a bleeding thing in a wind like this. I mean, what's normal is a wind strong like this would blow all my words clear away from you. You'd have this gesticulating figure, yes, that's all, outside your window, with a mouth running wild, but no words you could hear. Perfectly natural that, not to hear someone speaking outside your window in a wind strong like this. *(Pause)*
But my words can be heard, can't they?

(No response)

JACQUELINE: Yes, I think so. Each one. Like a bell.
   I think what must be happening in a wind strong like this is my words are getting carried, yes. Each one right there to where you sit. All my words is ringing, I bet, each one in your very ears. Like thoughts. You can hear your own thoughts. There's no wind what could blow away any of these thoughts.

(The wind continues.)

JACQUELINE: What's your name, dear? We might as well talk since we can hear each other so clear.

ARAMANDA: Aramanda.

JACQUELINE: Ah, Aramanda. It's nice, that name. Very nice, hmm. Aramanda. *(She taps on the window.)* Aramanda, then. If you could divide yourself into three parts, one part body, one part what's in the mind, and the last part is all the soul, what part, then, do you think will last the shortest? What part is the least of all these parts? Might be just the body. Right? What lasts the shortest. It's like straw. The barest whiff of wind can blow it away. Like it was never there.

(The wind continues.)

JACQUELINE: Hmm. Nice this wind. Must be picking up, I believe.

(She regards ARAMANDA.*)*

JACQUELINE: Oh, I'm sorry. Aramanda, then. I believe we were talking. And here I am saying everything again all to myself.
   Pah.
   What is it, then, you'd like to talk about, what last words, Aramanda, could be in store for you? What possible conversation?

ARAMANDA: Aramanda.

(Pause)

JACQUELINE: That's all? That's all you can tell me? Just your name? Aramanda?

(No response)

JACQUELINE: Hmm. Aramanda.
   You know, Aramanda, then. I believe the world's going to melt away someday. Yes. Vanish from our sight. Like it was never there. Just like what the Bible says. Mountains and hills will melt like wax. Drop, they will, and tumble to the sea, and the sea itself will be no more. Like what the Bible says.
   Do you read that book? What the Bible says?

ARAMANDA: Aramanda.

JACQUELINE: Yes, I can't either. Myself. Can't find my bleeding name anywhere in that book. Must be the

wrong book, I think. To be looking, I mean, for my
name. But I do like what it has to say. How all this
world and all its elements will melt. Tear, it will, right
down the middle. Fold up and go away. Like it never
was. Never did happen. And if this in the end never
did happen, all my words, all your body, all mountains
and seas, the teeth of lions, the heavens too which shall
pass away, what is it, then, that did happen? What's
left, do you think, after all this that didn't happen?

ARAMANDA: Aramanda.

JACQUELINE: Yes. It's like a thousand years out there,
Aramanda, then. One day is a thousand years, like a
watch in the night, and it doesn't take but a few such
days like that, right, Aramanda? To cancel all we
thought has happened?

(No response)

JACQUELINE: Looks like a wolf or something's been
eating you, Aramanda, then. Chunks are missing,
I can see, of flesh.
    Won't be feeling that body, I suspect, much longer.
It's being taken away from you. Like it never was.

(The wind is stronger.)

(The window sways back and forth.)

*(*JACQUELINE *holds onto her white hair.)*

JACQUELINE: It's looking somewhat flimsy, Aramanda.
Your wall here.

ARAMANDA: Crackle.

JACQUELINE: What was that?

ARAMANDA: Crackle.

JACQUELINE: I can't hear you anymore, I'm afraid, sorry,
Aramanda. Must be the wind.

ARAMANDA: Crackle.

JACQUELINE: It's picked up, you see, the wind. I'm not even sure how long your wall here can hold up in a wind getting stronger like this.

ARAMANDA: Crackle.

JACQUELINE: Looks like rain too. Hmm. All sorts of flooding, I can see, coming this way.

(The window falls to the ground.)

(A white wig blows off the head of JACQUELINE, *revealing dark hair and a face which is utterly male.)*

*(*ARAMANDA *stands up on one leg.)*

*(*JACQUELINE *approaches her.)*

(The sound of a creature walking across wet sand)

ARAMANDA: Crackle?

*(*JACQUELINE *continues his approach. Blackout)*

Scene Seven

(The big, blue space. A large crack passes indiscriminately through it.)

(The window hangs from above. Every pane is broken.)

*(*PRISCILLA *is unconscious in one of the chairs.)*

(The other chair has been overturned. PETER's *suitcase has been opened and its contents of balls, rings, clubs, and props strewn all across the floor. Papers from* PRISCILLA's *folder are scattered on the floor.)*

*(*PRISCILLA's *violin lies to one side, its neck broken.)*

(Enter PETER. *He carries a heavy shopping bag.)*

(He sees the room.)

PETER: Priscilla?

(PETER *puts the shopping bag down. He approaches*
PRISCILLA. *He kneels beside her.*)

PETER: Priscilla?

(No response)

(He inspects her.)

PETER: Come on, Priscilla. Don't do this to me. Wake up.

(PRISCILLA *stirs.* PETER *straightens her up in the chair.*)

PETER: Come on, Priscilla. What are you doing like this
in your chair? Let's get up, okay. Come on, Priscilla.

(PRISCILLA *remains in the chair, unconscious.*)

PETER: Priscilla?
   Priscilla, please, what happened here? In your room?

(No response)

(PETER *stands. He regards the room, seeing the broken
window for the first time. He picks up the second chair. He
places it next to* PRISCILLA *and sits. He takes* PRISCILLA's
head and places it against his shoulder. He strokes her hair.)

PETER: *(Softly)* Priscilla, I bought some paint. I bought
us paint and brushes too. So we could paint your gate.
You wanted a gate right there in your wall, Priscilla.
Remember where the wallpaper came down? You
wanted a gate?

(No response)

(PETER *sees the broken violin lying to one side.*)

PETER: *(Quietly)* Oh, my God.

(PETER *gently straightens* PRISCILLA *again in her chair.
He stands and crosses to the violin. He sits down on the
ground beside it. He holds its broken neck. He looks out front.*)

(The sound of a violin)

(A figure, SECOND PETER, *appears alone upstage. He juggles three balls.)*

(The sound of a chorus. Sounds of an orchestra)

(The violin continues.)

(Blackout)

END OF ACT ONE

ACT TWO

Scene One

(The big, blue space. The large crack has shifted to one side.)

(The window hangs from above. All the panes have been replaced.)

(The chairs stand side by side.)

(PETER's props have been returned to the suitcase. PRISCILLA's papers have been put back into the folder.)

(A gate hangs also now from above. PETER and PRISCILLA are painting it. On the ground between them is a can of paint.)

(The violin lies to one side, its neck still broken,)

(Pause)

PRISCILLA: Peter?

PETER: Hm?

PRISCILLA: Peter, I can't feel it again.

PETER: What, Priscilla? What don't you feel?

PRISCILLA: My body. It's gone.

PETER: Oh. *(Pause)* Would you like to stop, then?

PRISCILLA: I'm sorry?

PETER: Painting?

PRISCILLA: No.

PETER: You want to keep painting?

PRISCILLA: Yes.

PETER: Okay.

PRISCILLA: Yes. I want to paint.

PETER: Well, let's just rest, then. Okay, Priscilla?

PRISCILLA: Yes?

PETER: Uh huh. We'll rest right here. Till you can feel it better again. Your body.

(PETER *takes* PRISCILLA*'s paint brush. He puts the brushes in the can.)*

(Pause)

PETER: It's awfully pretty, Priscilla. Your body. I mean, for something you can't even feel sometimes.

PRISCILLA: *(Quietly)* It doesn't belong to me.

PETER: What?

PRISCILLA: It doesn't belong. Like it never was.

PETER: What doesn't belong? What never was? Your body?

PRISCILLA: I don't know.

PETER: It's not yours, that body? You just imagine it? That's why it's here?

PRISCILLA: I don't know.

PETER: Yeah? Well, you imagine something awful pretty, Priscilla.

PRISCILLA: It's not pretty.

PETER: It is to me. Always has been.

PRISCILLA: *(Abruptly)* I don't care, Peter, if it's pretty. *(She goes to a chair. She sits. She looks out at the crack in the big, blue space.)*

PETER: What's the matter, Priscilla? If I say it's pretty.

(No response)

PETER: What's the matter? Can't I clown anymore?
Really, Priscilla. Can't I tease?
I mean, I understand we have to stop once in a while,
for whatever reason, and wait for you, or your body,
whatever, to catch up again. I understand there's some
kind of mental slope going on here, and you need to
take these rests. No matter what simple thing we do.
But frankly, Priscilla, it would help, I'm sure, just to
smile a little. Give a little nod. Come on, Priscilla, nod
for me. Break out into a grin. Beam. I want to see you
beam for me.

(PRISCILLA *gives a smile.)*

PETER: That's better, yeah. I like it, I do, Priscilla.
When you break out. You beam a little for me.
(Pause) You feel it again?
It's come back to you? Your body?

(PRISCILLA *gives a nod.)*

PETER: I'm going to paint, okay? Paint a little more of
this gate. You come and join me. When you're ready.
(He takes a brush out of the can. He paints.)

(PRISCILLA *watches.)*

PETER: You know, I think of you as a scout, I do.
Whatever mental slope this is you're climbing, I feel
I'm going to have to do it too, yes, someday. I'm going
to have to stop looking around like this in a body,
looking to this world we live to keep me happy.
In fact, I think of you as a scout for all the rest of us.
Everybody back here in the world. Because, frankly,
there's got to be some kind of mental slope out of here.
Out of this place we got left somehow to die.
And I can imagine, yes. A scout must get astounded
sometimes. Scared. All alone up there. Seeing what the

rest of us have yet to see. What we will have to see too.
When we finally have no choice left, no more excuses.
But to catch up to you.

(PRISCILLA *stands. She goes to* PETER. *She takes the paint
brush from him.*)

PRISCILLA: Peter. I know it seems, to you, I'm sort of
some scout. I see what's up ahead. A whole kingdom,
I suppose, within. A place we have to get to, right,
without our bodies?
   And I'm sorry. To give such an impression.
   Because, Peter, I watch you sometimes. I do. And
I don't feel ahead. No. I'm left behind. I can't believe
how far you've gone on. How grand you look to me.
How safe. How sound. And when you take my hand
sometimes I feel I could open a door. There's a door,
right there, in front of me. Within my grasp. Where
I can come in. From all the rain and all the flood out
there. And I feel windows too. Places to look out. A
view. Where I can see the world from how you can see.
I can see a man. And a woman too. I can see everything
that should have been there up ahead for us. (*Pause*)
You shouldn't come back like this. I shouldn't keep
calling you back like this.

PETER: You're not calling me back, Priscilla. At all.

(PETER *reaches for* PRISCILLA'*s hand which holds the paint
brush. He takes her hand and guides the brush along the gate.*)

PETER: You know, Priscilla. I've reached out and
touched several people. In this life of mine. Reached
all the way over there and touched what I could see
of them. Brought them as close as I could.
   But never, I guess, have I ever felt as close as I felt
when close to you. And all I did was take your hand.
That's how close we were, Priscilla. Taking hands.

(PETER *lets go of* PRISCILLA'*s hand. She continues to paint
the gate.*)

(The sound of a violin)

(Lights dim.)

(A figure, SECOND PRISCILLA, *appears beyond the gate. She is juggling rings.)*

(The sound of a chorus. Sounds of an orchestra)

(Blackout)

Scene Two

(A forest. The forest seems darker. There is a second crack now.)

(The window and a partially painted gate hang from above.)

*(*COQUELICOT *sits in a chair. She is wearing* PRISCILLA's *dress. She has lost an arm and one wing is still broken. The other wing lies in her lap.)*

(Nearby are the other chair, PETER's *suitcase, and a broken violin.)*

*(*JACQUELINE *stands outside the window. He walks back and forth. He straightens his wig.)*

(He goes to the gate. He regards it. He regards COQUELICOT *through the gate.)*

JACQUELINE: *(To* COQUELICOT*)* Did you do this? Is this your gate?

(No response)

JACQUELINE: Seems a strange thing to do to me. Paint this gate on a wall.
   Whoever heard of painting a gate on a wall? Walls is for wallpaper.
Or pictures. Pretty little pictures of houses and family, all sorts of pets, pictures, yes, of nature, that's what should be going on here on a wall.

Not somebody painting like this a gate. *(He turns sideways. He measures himself, and his large dress, against the gate.)* Seems awful narrow to me, this gate. Much too narrow, I bet, way too straight, to be of any use at all, yes, in this wall.

(JACQUELINE steps away from the gate. He regards COQUELICOT.)

JACQUELINE: I hate to have to do this, but would you mind, once again, telling me what it is your name?

COQUELICOT: Coquelicot.

JACQUELINE: Ah, yes. That's it, of course. Coquelicot, then. It's very nice, I think, that. For a name.

(The sound of a breeze in the woods)

(He lifts his face. He breathes the air.)

(The stage darkens.)

JACQUELINE: Awful nice in here, Coquelicot, then. What a lovely forest. All this forest you have. In your head. *(Pause)* It's dark, though, isn't it? Having a forest like this can get dark. Amazing how dark sometimes. It can get in a forest.

What's amazing also to me is how clear I must appear to you. How distinct you look to me. How the eyes adjust. What they get used to. I mean, you'd think what's normal in a darkness like this is I would be all blurred. Just some dark shadow, that's all, lapping at your window. *(Pause)* I've been wondering Coquelicot, then. Did you happen to hear what happened to Aramanda?

(No response)

JACQUELINE: Or are you not aware? Of our little Aramanda, then? What used to live in the first house. On my way to here. *(He taps on the window.)* Coquelicot, then. Tell me. If you could divide yourself into three parts, one part body, one the mind, and the last part all the soul, what part, then, do you think will last the middle? What part is the second part of all these parts? Might be the mind. Right? What lasts the middle. It's like sticks, I think. Yes. A good firm gust of wind could blow them sticks all away. Like they was never there.

(JACQUELINE *continues to regard* COQUELICOT *through the window.*)

JACQUELINE: Pah. It's horrible these days.
 How I find myself all alone like this. Talking to myself.

(Sound of a breeze getting stronger)

JACQUELINE: I bet, however, I know one thing we could talk about. Yes, in this forest. I bet we could talk about your friend. What he wanted you to read for him. In that folder. What I see right there. Lying on a trunk.
 Would you like that, Coquelicot, then?
 If I tell what's in that folder? If I speak to you all the hand-writing in there?

COQUELICOT: Coquelicot.

JACQUELINE: I thought so, yes. I knew it could please you no end, yes, to tell our friend what's in our folder. All our harmless stories.
 So why don't you pass it to me, then? That folder. What's lying there on the trunk. Pass it to me right now through this window. So I can read to you.

COQUELICOT: Coquelicot.

JACQUELINE: That's right, good Coquelicot, then.

(COQUELICOT *stands. She picks up the folder on* PETER's *trunk. She goes to the window. She hands the folder to* JACQUELINE *through the window.*)

(JACQUELINE *opens the folder.*)

JACQUELINE: Hmm. Lovely. It looks so lovely to me. All these words in here. All this handwriting. *(He turns*

a page.) Ah, yes. It's about a wolf.
  Did you know that?

COQUELICOT: Coquelicot?

JACQUELINE: Yes, Coquelicot, then. All about a wolf in
here. What he says. How he thinks. And this wolf, it
claims in here, is not what we all believe got boiled in
a pot of water at the foot of a chimney and all the pigs
went dancing.
  No, that's not what's here. No wolf like that.
  No, the wolf in here is much more, I think, than can
meet the eye. What could boil in water. What could be
contained in a simple story like that about what is good
and what is evil. All taking place in some literal world.
Some fantastic land where people believe what they can
see.
  What kind of land is that?
  Where all the wolves is out there? Where we can see.
(He turns a page.) Hmm. It's talking here about what are
internal wolves. What's in our midst. A wolf in here
more relative. It's saying we should always look to who
the author is. Who is it telling. And not just the story.
It says here what could look to the naked eye like a pig
living nice and peaceful in a lovely brick house could
actually be the wolf. Heh. It's a wolf in there living
nice and peaceful in a lovely brick house. He's telling
a story, yes, to all our children. *(He turns a page.)*

(The sound of wind. A wolfs howls.)

JACQUELINE: Hmm. It's very stirring, don't you think?
What's in this folder.
  I mean, the implications of this are immense. That a
story, where we killed the wolf, is actually being told to
us by the wolf that was killed. Now, I mean, either the
wolf is killed and that's the story, and we shouldn't be
building any house of straw and sticks. We have a place
of bricks to go to. Or else the wolf isn't killed. And we
have no house at all of bricks to go. Because if the wolf

isn't killed, then who can be telling this story he was
killed, except a wolf who wants us to think he's killed.
A wolf who is bluffing. Who came to our door and we
let him in. And once he's in, there's really no wall left,
is there, between us and any story he could please
himself to tell.

   It's like the fox wearing the livery of a hen. The devil
aping God. I mean, this is elementary. It's easy breaking
into houses. Yes. When you get yourself invited in.
And if the wolf's already invited in, I can see no sense
either running off to that brick house we were told.

(JACQUELINE *closes the folder. He hands it back through the*
window.)

(COQUELICOT *reaches for it.* JACQUELINE *takes*
COQUELICOT's *wrist as she grasps the folder.)*

JACQUELINE: *(Holding* COQUELICOT's *wrist)* Quiet.
You seem awful quiet to me.
   What is it, then? Making you so quiet?

(The stage darkens.)

JACQUELINE: Listening, are you, then? That's it. For
some still voice? Some angel of the air? To lead you
out of here?

(No response)

JACQUELINE: I can't stand like this when a person
doesn't answer to me.

(JACQUELINE *twists* COQUELICOT's *wrist. The sound of a*
bone snapping. COQUELICOT *cries out as* JACQUELINE *forces*
her to the ground.)

(The wind is stronger. A wolf howls again.)

(The window sways as JACQUELINE *leans through it.)*

JACQUELINE: It all comes back in the end, Coquelicot,
then. To the house which was built, you know, on rock.
And the other, what was built on sand.

Because I do believe, long ago, in the days when
they thought this world was flat, some millennia ago,
I believe there was indeed, once upon a time, a house
you could build on rock. A very kingdom, yes, within.
Separate from all this world without.

But that rock, whatever it is, that kingdom got
covered long ago by what is all around us now. By all
this vast expanse we have, all this world, yes, of sand.

(The window and JACQUELINE's *wig blow to the ground.)*

COQUELICOT: Crackle?

*(*JACQUELINE *drags* COQUELICOT *across the stage.)*

(The sound of a creature walking across wet sand.)

(Blackout)

Scene Three

(The big, blue space. The cracks are gone.)

(The window and gate hang down from above.)

*(*JACQUELINE *sits in a chair. His wig is gone. He wears*
PRISCILLA's *dress.)*

(Nearby are the other chair, PETER's *suitcase, and a broken
violin.)*

(Enter PETER.*)*

PETER: Hi.

*(*JACQUELINE *smiles.)*

PETER: You okay?

(No response)

PETER: You know, something came back to me. Outside.
Something you said one time. Probably you don't even
remember, but I remember. Because what you could
say was so frustrating to me. So ludicrous. How you

would have these thoughts sometimes, an idea, the very moment when all I wanted ever to do was just to kiss you. *(Pause)* You were like a child. Questions bubbled up in you. Asking, like a child, if this is a dream? Some kind of sleep, that's all, the world we live? These things we're saying, right now, in the end if they never were. Never did happen.

Until I didn't know myself anymore. How to respond. Except to get out of the way. Decide, finally, to take off. Let you ask yourself this stuff without me trying all the time to stop you. *(Pause)* What came to me outside just now was how you told me one time you could feel, deep down, how this body, yours, was nothing but a veil. That's right. A covering. And I said, Come on, your body isn't a veil. It covers what? And you said this thing, you said, Your view of God. And I said, Oh, yeah? Your view of God? You'd see God, would you, if you had no body, no veil like this, if you were invisible, that's what you'd see? God?

And you said, Yes. That's what you could decide to see.

Whereas I said, I'm not so sure what I might decide to see. Beyond this body. In a big, blue yonder. What's invisible. I might see, finally, what's opposed to God. What lurks behind the bushes. The adversary. *(Pause)* That's what came back to me. That conversation. What I said to you. Right before I left. *(He sits in the other chair.)*

JACQUELINE: Surprised to see me, aren't you?

PETER: Hm?

JACQUELINE: Thought I was still outside.

PETER: No. I thought you were here.

JACQUELINE: What?

PETER: In here.

JACQUELINE: Oh, funny. Yes. And I thought I was outside, heh, heh. Imagine.

(Pause)

PETER: I didn't know you were outside. You should have told me. *(Pause)* Where have you been, then? Outside.

(Pause)

JACQUELINE: What are you looking at?

PETER: Hm?

JACQUELINE: You seem to be looking at something.

PETER: I'm sorry. I was thinking.

JACQUELINE: Ah.

PETER: That's all.

JACQUELINE: I'm thinking too, it's good, I think, to be thinking. Would you like to know what it is, then? That I'm thinking?

PETER: Yes?

JACQUELINE: Good. Because I'm thinking if you were to describe your friend Priscilla to someone, say what's important to you about her, all her qualities, what might it be, then, you think you'd say?
    Eh? About Priscilla?

(Pause)

PETER: I'd say her honesty.

JACQUELINE: What?

PETER: That's right. Your honesty.

JACQUELINE: What honesty?

PETER: How you're willing, that's all, to look within yourself. That's what I'd say. This inner vision you have. This constant need. To see behind what you assume. *(Pause)* You seem surprised.

JACQUELINE: Hm?

PETER: To hear honesty.

JACQUELINE: Yes. Yes, that quite surprises me.

PETER: Why? What would you have said?

JACQUELINE: About Priscilla?

PETER: Yes. How would you describe yourself? To a friend?

(Pause)

JACQUELINE: I'd describe her as hard to capture, myself.

PETER: Hard to capture?

JACQUELINE: Yes. It's no easy matter, no, capturing the likes of Priscilla.

(Pause)

PETER: I agree.

JACQUELINE: Do you really?

PETER: Yes, she's hard to capture. Hard to describe. Hard to ever know what to assume about Priscilla. I mean I once assumed, for example, all your beliefs were foolish.

JACQUELINE: What beliefs?

PETER: Well, that we shouldn't get to know each other. Physically, I mean. That sort of belief.

JACQUELINE: Really?

PETER: Yes, that's what you believed.

JACQUELINE: Amazing.

PETER: Hm?

JACQUELINE: It's amazing what a belief can do.

PETER: Yes, you thought we better be married. I mean, to get to know each other like that.

JACQUELINE: *(To himself)* Oh, my dear.

PETER: And so I thought, great, this is what has to be. I'll get married. Be like that for her, man and wife.

JACQUELINE: Oh, my, my.

PETER: But I shouldn't have assumed that, it seems.

JACQUELINE: Assumed what?

PETER: Well, that you wanted, that's all, to get married.

JACQUELINE: Ah, yes.
  Well, it's hard, as I say. To capture Priscilla.

(Pause)

PETER: Yes. Capture. I think that's a good word. You seem terribly afraid sometimes. Of capture. Something about you could be captured. Some spirit in the body. And one way to look at this is to think this is crazy. This woman is crazy. Who is it that has traumatized her in such a way that she thinks she could be captured by her own body?
  It's ludicrous.
  But then I watch you. The things you used to do. How you used to practice all the time. You played that violin. How you could perform, and I would see, yes, she's right. I can see what's spirit there. What's innocent. Wants to break out free. I see how lovely. How you long for all of an open space out there. How you reach out all the way to the end of where your body will go, out there beyond any grasp. And I see myself following you. See these glimpses, watching you, of what a body could never express. I hear words. Some sort of singing in words. And I hear myself singing. I sing words when I watch you. Hear words in my mouth I could never

express. *(He suddenly stands. He goes to the window.
He looks out.)*

(He looks back at JACQUELINE.*)*

PETER: It doesn't surprise me sometimes, Priscilla.
To see you under such an assault.

JACQUELINE: An assault?

PETER: Yes, there's some crisis. Obviously. Some battle
to get you.
    And I get nervous. Sometimes I'm nervous just
speaking each word I speak to you. *(He steps away
from the window.)*

JACQUELINE: Well, that's rather silly. Getting nervous
like that. Speaking words to me. Because, frankly,
there's nothing at all for you to be nervous. Nothing
to see.

*(A crack appears in the big, blue space. In the crack can be
seen* PRISCILLA*'s dark outline.)*

JACQUELINE: Hmm. Looks like it's about to break apart
again. Out there. *(He stands. He goes to the window. He
looks out.)*

(He looks back at PETER.*)*

JACQUELINE: Speaking of glimpses. Tell me. Do you
think within each one of us is a wolf?

PETER: A wolf?

JACQUELINE: Yes, tell me.

PETER: What sort of wolf?

JACQUELINE: Just a wolf, that's all. Any sort.

PETER: I don't know.

JACQUELINE: You've never looked a person in the eye
and thought, that's a wolf I see in there?

PETER: I don't know.

JACQUELINE: Oh, come on.

PETER: Sure, I suppose I've seen such a wolf.

JACQUELINE: Yes?

PETER: On occasion, sure.

(Pause)

JACQUELINE: How about now?

PETER: Hm?

JACQUELINE: Can you see what's a wolf in me?

PETER: No. I could never see a wolf in you.

JACQUELINE: Why ever not?

PETER: It's not anything I could imagine. A wolf in you.

JACQUELINE: How about when I'm really silent? Dark, let's say, and brooding. Any such glimpses then, you think, of a wolf in me?

PETER: No. No such glimpse I can remember.

(Pause)

JACQUELINE: Hmm. I think there's wolves in all of us. Even you.

PETER: You think I got a wolf in me?

JACQUELINE: Oh, yes. Something wolfish, I bet.

PETER: What would that be?

JACQUELINE: You don't know yourself?

PETER: I'm just asking what you've noticed.

JACQUELINE: About the wolf in you?

PETER: Yes.

JACQUELINE: Ah. Well, it seems to me that your wolf is not just a regular wolf.

PETER: No?

JACQUELINE: Yes, we're both quite the dandies, aren't we?

PETER: Dandies?

JACQUELINE: Yes, I mean, all this primping and prancing. In what is sheep's clothing. All this honesty you claim. Inner vision. This need to look behind what we assume. That's just a cover-up we have. It's clothing. All this layer of stuff on top, hiding from view, how ravenous we have always been. Rapacious. I mean, for what could be between us. This force, I feel, pressure all the time. Like gravitation. Keeping us gravitated to each other on this earth. *(Pause)* Well, don't look so startled. I've given some thought to this. I told you I've been thinking. And what I think is I come from a long line of wolf. I mean, what's a wolf inside. A long line of that. From mother to son, son to his daughter, and on and on like that could last forever. What I feel for you could last us here forever. *(Pause)* If I were to describe Priscilla to someone, I'd have to mention, I'm afraid, her desire to kill the wolf in her. Stop all this long line. Keep it at bay. Can you imagine? Kill what is natural in her. I mean, most people, they accept a little wolf in their life. A little wolf is what can bring people together. Give us picnics and boating parties, all because of a little wolf, what got them started.

That's what amazes me about Priscilla. Trying to chase away like this her natural wolf. Which makes me think what's a little wolf to all of us, what's a nice excitement, is something big and bad to her. Quite grievous. What may have mauled her once. Come upon her as a child. Pulled the wings off a young woman. What's a little wolf to us, what keeps us happy, she saw take apart her body. She got a peek, a glimpse, of all the big, bad land, what's lurking there, behind our very body.

But I do think, still, it's no use fighting like this any wolf. A wolf's not so big when you don't fight. He can be just a tiny part, that's all, in your life, a slight hunger, what's in the background, yes, what's hardly even noticed, if you do not fight it. Keep a wolf like this at bay.

(Pause)

PETER: Why are you talking like this?

JACQUELINE: Like what?

PETER: Like you're speaking for Priscilla.

JACQUELINE: Who else can speak for Priscilla?

PETER: No, you keep using the third person.

JACQUELINE: What person?

PETER: As if you're separate from Priscilla.

JACQUELINE: But that's my point. My point all along. I do not have to be separate at all from Priscilla.

PETER: No, why are you talking as if Priscilla isn't here?

JACQUELINE: Because she isn't here.

PETER: No? Then why are you here?

JACQUELINE: Because I've come here. For Priscilla.

PETER: What, if you're Priscilla and Priscilla isn't here?

(Pause)

JACQUELINE: I can see you understand nothing. You understand nothing to do with Priscilla. *(He takes a crumpled piece of paper out of his pocket.)* I believe this paper's yours. What's crumpled here in my pocket.

(JACQUELINE flicks the paper over to PETER.)

JACQUELINE: All the names, what's on that list, it's all mine. It's all come to me. Each little name in there is what I've met along my path.

Including your name.
I've seen it, yes, your name. Right there. On that list.

(PETER *picks up the paper.*)

JACQUELINE: My name is Jacqueline. You can call me
Jacq.

(*A second crack appears in the big, blue space.*)

JACQUELINE: Now can you see the wolf in me?
What's been lurking all the time?

(*No response*)

(JACQUELINE *picks up the broken violin.*)

(*The sound of a gentle breeze*)

JACQUELINE: Do you like these birds? All the birds you
see flying in the air? On this dress I wear?

(*No response*)

(*The stage darkens.*)

JACQUELINE: Can you see Priscilla now?
   How she's standing here. Right before your eyes.
In this lovely dress?
   All the birds upon this dress. Beckoning.

(*Sound of a breeze getting stronger*)

JACQUELINE: And below all the birds is these shoes.
Priscilla's feet. What's in these shoes. What you see
walk like dancing. Seen tapping when she plays the
violin here.

(*The sound of wind*)

JACQUELINE: But it's her eyes, isn't it? Above all the
birds in this world is her eyes. How they look to you.
How she calls. And all this world between can vanish.
Yes, if you just reach out, right now, your hands, and
take this moment.

(The wind is stronger. A wolf howls.)

(The dark outline of PRISCILLA *in the first crack stirs.)*

JACQUELINE: Come. Fill your hands right here.

PRISCILLA'S VOICE: Peter?

JACQUELINE: Feel a wind rise, strong and furious in you.

PRISCILLA'S VOICE: No, Peter?

JACQUELINE: What's been held back in you all these years. The heart and soul of what you really want.

(The wind is furious.)

*(*PRISCILLA *steps out of the crack. She comes downstage.)*

(A wolf screams at her.)

PRISCILLA: No, Peter.

JACQUELINE: *(Continuing to* PETER*)*...Feel it break out and rain in you. Feel the flood rise up...

PRISCILLA: Peter, no. Listen.

JACQUELINE: ...all the fury grip you like a vast current, carry you faraway from any land, until you are free and wild again...

PETER: *(Seeing* PRISCILLA*)* Priscilla?

JACQUELINE: ....like the beast you are to bite and devour!...

PRISCILLA: Yes, Peter.

(The big, blue space cracks open once again, throwing PETER *into darkness.)*

*(*JACQUELINE *turns on* PRISCILLA. *The window falls to the ground.)*

(The sound of a wolf tearing at something)

*(*JACQUELINE *grabs* PRISCILLA *by the neck. He forces her to the ground and stands over her.)*

(The wind begins to abate.)

JACQUELINE: I found my way, didn't I, my dear? Into your brick house. I just followed the names right there. On that list. Till I got to the name of your friend there. That's what let me in. Your friend. All that you feel for your friend.

(Pause)

JACQUELINE: Hmm. Gone quiet again, I see.
   It's amazing how quiet it gets in here.
   I can't stand it like this when you're quiet. What did I tell you about going quiet like this on me?

(No response)

JACQUELINE: Listening, are you, then? That's it. For some still voice? Some angel of the air? To lead you out of here? Some sign of a kingdom within? Some other house you might live?
   Is that what's making it all so quiet here?
   Heh heh.

(No response)

JACQUELINE: Hmm. I can see no kingdom within. No other house. Here we are, you and I, this very moment, in a land beyond all lands of body, and I can hear no little voice of spirit. There's nothing pure and simple God has made. No kingdom within to conquer all this big, bad world without.
   It's just you and me, that's all, my dear. Yes. In this within.

(JACQUELINE twists PRISCILLA's neck. The sound of something snapping.)

JACQUELINE: It all goes back to the tempter, I think. What took Christ to the wilderness mountain. And showed him all the kingdoms of this world in a moment of time.

And it's very nice, isn't it, how Christ refused this world, because this world wasn't his world to be king of. He had another world, didn't he? Our little kingdom within. A house built on rock.

Very nice, yes.

And it's amazing to me, it is, to watch all these Christians go out themselves to conquer now all this world he refused. Into every land, every nook and cranny, all the little Christians have sent their warriors, all their merchants, what they teach, all of it still out there trying to conquer what's left to conquer in this world.

All their lands out there of body.

Heh.

Sounds like that rock turned into bread. The bread of this world. Sounds like we tossed ourselves off the pinnacle, didn't we?

(JACQUELINE *twists* PRISCILLA's *neck. The sound of something snapping*)

JACQUELINE: It's like I said. There's no pig in any brick house. It's a wolf himself in there.

So what's the sense left to all this quiet? This listening, then. For some way to lift up yourself out of here. Beyond my grasp.

You should be howling right now. Loud and clear, yes, as I approach. Make my advance on what's left of you. Come, Priscilla. Howl with me. Let us howl together in the huge dark of night. In this chaos we can howl together. There's no need anymore to be separate like this.

(The sound of wind is gone.)

(JACQUELINE *regards* PRISCILLA.*)

JACQUELINE: Hm. What is it makes it so quiet here? I can't stand it quiet like this. I've told you. *(Pause)* Thoughts can be disturbing in a quiet such as this

is quiet. *(Pause)* Listening, then? For some still voice?
Some angel of the air? To lead you out of here? Some
sign of a kingdom within? Some other home you might
live?

(Pause)

(PRISCILLA *stands.)*

PRISCILLA: You repeat yourself.

JACQUELINE: Hm?

PRISCILLA: I've never heard that before. How you repeat
yourself.

JACQUELINE: I repeat myself? Is there something wrong,
then? To repeat myself.

PRISCILLA: *(Realizing)* This is not home.

JACQUELINE: Heh?

PRISCILLA: You are not my home.

JACQUELINE: What's not, my dear, your home?

PRISCILLA: Any place you could enter. That's not my
home. *(She steps out of the room.)*

JACQUELINE: *(Unaware)* Oh, really? Not your home?
What I could enter? Well, that's quite remarkable
indeed. Because I can see no other home, no other
house left anywhere all around, except this one right
here. Where I have indeed entered. That's what I see.
It's all that I see.

(PRISCILLA *continues to walk outside the room.)*

(JACQUELINE *prowls, unseeing, inside the room.)*

JACQUELINE: Is there something else, then? That you
see?

(No response)

JACQUELINE: And where is it, then? This something else.
What you see.

(No response)

JACQUELINE: You're not going to tell me? Not going
to show proof, then? Of what you see? Some little
glimpse, maybe, of proof?
   Or are you just going afflict me? With this quiet.
Because you are afraid I may mock it. Your proof.
Huff and puff it down. All over again. Each proof.
   Pah!
   This is what makes you so quiet. That's it, then.
Some notion. The paltry thought. I'm not your home.
Where you live.

(A silhouette of a large horse has appeared upstage.)

(JACQUELINE sees the horse.)

JACQUELINE: What's that? What's that horse over there?
Is that your horse?

(The silhouette of the horse upstage moves. It comes to a stop.)

JACQUELINE: I asked you, Is that your horse? Are you
leaving here on that horse?

(PRISCILLA remains quiet.)

JACQUELINE: You better tell me about this horse.
What is it you'll do. On that horse.

(Pause)

PRISCILLA: You never touched him. My friend.

JACQUELINE: What?

PRISCILLA: That's my friend's horse. You never got close.

JACQUELINE: Oh, yes, I am. Very close. I felt him listen.
With all his heart. To what you feel for him. Like
gravitation.

PRISCILLA: But you don't speak for me.

JACQUELINE: What?

PRISCILLA: You never did.

JACQUELINE: Of course I speak for you. All the time.
I hear it loud and clear. What you know is true. Makes
sense. What you've seen, oh, yes, with your own very
eyes. What you have witnessed. From the day you were
born. All the wolf you have seen. In a house built on
rock. All the cracks right here. You see across the sky.

PRISCILLA: It's not your business. What I see.

JACQUELINE: Not my business?

PRISCILLA: Nor do you speak for me.

JACQUELINE: Is this what you have to say? After all this
time? It's not my business?
   Is this what you hope, then? Your last words to me?
It's not my business?

(Pause)

(The silhouette of the horse upstage moves again. It stops.)

JACQUELINE: I don't like it like this, I don't.
   When I find myself fumble. For words. What made
us so close, so dear. Our thoughts. *(Pause)* What is it
you do, when you get quiet like this? I'd like to know
in this quiet is there something I could hear? Would
you tell? Some little word. What might really speak?
Some land you might dwell?

(The cracks in the big, blue space have begun to fade.)

(PRISCILLA watches them.)

PRISCILLA: *(Softly)* Crackle. The cracks are going.

(She regards JACQUELINE.)

PRISCILLA: It's hard to believe it now. How afraid you
made me.
   All this time.

How much sense you made. How your words could sound. Like my very own thoughts. What I want.
Or fear.

(Pause)

PRISCILLA: I no longer fear what you could make me do. All your actions. How you lurk in the background. Your huge past. All your heredity. How hard you were to understand.

Because I can see you now. All of you. Out here in the open. I can hear you too. Each thing you want. All that you could have ever done to me.

I see how far you've travelled, how desperate, to follow each step I take out of this world.

(The horse moves again. It stops.)

PRISCILLA: I'm going back now to see my friend. He's waiting for me. *(Pause. She picks up the violin.)* I know I will see you again. Hear you many times still.

But you are no longer in front of me. You are what's behind.

(The sound of a violin)

PRISCILLA: You could not possibly dwell, ever, in any land where I will go.

(Blackout)

(The violin continues.)

Scene Four

(The soft sound of a violin still playing)

(A large, empty blue space)

(The window frame with pale curtains hangs down from above.)

(There are two empty chairs.)

(PRISCILLA *appears. She comes to the window. She pauses.*
She goes to one of the chairs. She sits.)

(*Enter* PETER. *He carries a large, black suitcase, or trunk.*
He sets the suitcase down. He looks at PRISCILLA.)

PETER: That's very beautiful, Priscilla.

(*No response*)

PETER: That dress. I like it very much. (*Pause*) I still
can't get over the birds flying. All those birds in the air.
On your dress.

(PRISCILLA *smiles.*)

PRISCILLA: Peter?

PETER: Yes, Priscilla?

PRISCILLA: I'm glad you're back.

PETER: Good.

(PRISCILLA *stands.*)

PRISCILLA: It's lovely, Peter. The things you say.

(PRISCILLA *goes to* PETER.)

PRISCILLA: I feel I could wait sometimes forever, Peter.
Go through a second death, even. Just to come back and
hear the things you say.

(PRISCILLA *takes* PETER *by the hand. She holds his hand.*)

(*Lights dim.*)

(*Two figures,* SECOND PETER *and* SECOND PRISCILLA,
appear upstage. They dance together, passing clubs between
them.)

(*The sound of a chorus. Sounds of an orchestra. The violin*
continues.)

(*Blackout*)

END OF PLAY

www.ingramcontent.com/pod-product-compliance
Lightning Source LLC
Chambersburg PA
CBHW070026110426
42741CB00034B/2608